Wedding Favors

& decorations

MW00710464

QUARRY

THE ARTFUL
BRIDE

Wedding Favors

& decorations

A STYLISH BRIDE'S GUIDE TO SIMPLE, HANDMADE WEDDING CRAFTS

GLOUCESTER MASSACHUSETTS

QUARRY BOOKS

APRIL L. PAFFRATH, PAULA GRASDAL & LIVIA MCREE

© 2004 by Quarry Books

All rights reserved. No part of this book may be reproduced in any form without written persion of the copyright owners. All images in this book have been reproduced with the knowledge and prior consent of the artists concerned, and no responsibility is accepted by producer, publisher, or printer for any infringement of copyright or otherwise, arising from the contents of this publication. Every effort has been made to ensure that credits accurately comply with information supplied.

First published in the USA by

Quarry Books, a member of the

Quayside Publishing Group

33 Commercial Street

Gloucester, Massachusetts 01930-5089

Telephone: (978) 282-9590

Fax: (978) 283-2742

www.quarrybooks.com

Library of Congress Cataloging-in-Publication Data

Paffrath, April L.

The artful bride : wedding favors and decorations : a stylish bride's guide to simple, handmade wedding crafts / April L. Paffrath and Laura McFadden.

p. cm.

Includes bibliographical references.

ISBN 1-59253-039-7 (pbk.)

1. Handicraft. 2. Wedding decorations. I. McFadden, Laura. II. Title.

TT149.P36 2004

745.594'1—dc22   2003023176

CIP

ISBN-13: 978-1-59253-039-7

ISBN-10: 1-59253-039-7

10 9 8 7 6 5 4 3

Design: Laura McFadden

Layout and Production: Susan Raymond

Cover Image: Bobbie Bush Photography, www.bobbiebush.com

Printed in USA

Contents

Introduction

A celebration sounds like fun. Whether it's dancing far into the night (or morning), a feast for the masses, or candlelight and sophisticated ambiance, you want everyone to be filled with joy and to share in the excitement. Too often, a celebration can become overwhelming if you're the one throwing it and organizing all the details. Let's face it, it can take a lot of work to give the impression of fun. A little stress is livable—we know you deal with a modicum of pressure with your usual panache every day of your stylish life. Navigating normal tensions is par for the course of modern lives. However, head too far down the path of managing minutia, and the enjoyment begins to fizzle. Why give equal weight to every single element of a wedding, anyway? Details are only charming and enjoyable when they don't take over your life, so keep a level head and don't try to do it all. It is possible to keep it fun. After all, there is little sense in spending as much energy on napkin rings as you do on the guest list. Reigning in obsessive tendencies will go a long way to ensure a positive experience as you prepare for the wedding. Details and crafts are a great way to leave your mark—let it be a vivacious, happy, and calm one. It's all about creating an experience and having fun—through the planning *and* partying process.

It comes as no surprise, we're sure, that weddings are a prime example of complicated enjoyment—it looks like sweetness and light, but it can take hours of reworking (and overworking) the details to get everything right. The appearance of happenstance or coincidental details—that everything is falling together "just so" as if it were a happy accident—takes loads of attention, control, and practice. You have to be wise and figure out what is really worth it. Make elements for your wedding that mean something to you—but don't over-commit to a craft.

Why do some brides get a reputation for lacking humor as they plan their weddings? We can't be sure, but we have a suspicion is has something to do with hand-embossing every piece of paper with the image of a flower. What happens when you do that? You're forced to carry the embossing through to everything, lest it all look unfinished; you give up your time and conversation to make sure it gets done; and, what started as a nice gesture of spring has become a demanding floral beast. We want you to let yourself off the hook. Crafts are not supposed to make you edgy or rubber stamp–crazed. Quite the opposite. Making items for your wedding celebration can give you some automatic quiet time—some chance to sit, focused on one task instead of juggling a million things. It lets you connect with your spouse-to-be and your guests, too. Planning ahead and sticking to your ideas will help prevent you from overdoing it.

Making something by hand is a thoughtful gesture. But that doesn't mean you have to do everything yourself. There is a reason why there are so many wedding industry professionals around—because it is difficult for one person to do it all. For all the elements you make by hand, you are probably saving money—but you are spending something else just as valuable: your time and energy. You need to decide from the get-go how much money, time, and energy you have in your budget. Be realistic about how much of these three resources will be spent on each element. Spend too much of any of them and your enjoyment suffers, and so does that of many of your closest cohorts. It's all about balance.

Remember that while planning a wedding, there will be dinners, cocktails, picnics, and parties that crop up. Don't overschedule yourself and miss out on the good things in life. Take on what is special to you and leave the rest to professionals, wedding planners, a group of talented friends, and mail order. Try to limit the handmade items to things that cannot be purchased, or that you would have to go without for budgetary reasons.

It will be a breeze to incorporate your inimitable style into your wedding. The guests already know and like you. They know your kooky taste in color combinations, your penchant for salsa music, and the ever present yellow flowers at your house. Don't let them down. A formal occasion does not mean you rewrite your personality—it means you amplify it and suit the event to fit.

We've given you options here for unique celebration ideas. Dress up a table, direct people to their seats, decorate the area, and amuse people. A good way to tackle it? Read the directions and go. A better way? Look through the projects and adapt them to fit you. We've avoided showing examples in the lacy white floral style—not because it is ill suited for these projects, but because you've probably seen enough of that to adequately adapt to that look if it's your bag. If it's not, we've given you a head start on a pleasant, modern deviation.

Lucky in Love Treats

PEARLY CHOCOLATE FAVORS

Sweetness is a theme for the day. A wedding can be a casual affair, a formal mass, or a party until dawn. All forms, though, obviously contain expressions of love. Echo that sweet sentiment without getting syrupy. Chocolates are sophisticated, and they are familiar elements in courtship (chocolates on Valentine's Day, bon-bons after a date), but they are still plenty of fun for both young children and adults. Make a twist on a traditional gift by dusting the molded chocolates with luster powder, a food-safe confectioner's supply that is made to give sweets a jewel-like finish.

DIRECTIONS

1. Prepare packaging first by cutting a piece of corrugated paper board to fit your candy bags. Press foil over board and trim excess. Slip board into candy bag and set aside.

2. Melt chocolate tablets in double boiler or microwave (follow directions on package).

3. Spoon chocolate into candy mold.

4. Tap mold to even out the chocolate and get rid of air bubbles.

5. Let cool until set. (You can put it in the refrigerator for 10 to 15 minutes if you're in a hurry.)

6. Pop chocolates out of molds and arrange faceup on a clean surface. Wear gloves to protect the candies from fingerprints and melting.

TIP *Too much hassle to melt and mold chocolate? (It's really very easy, though.) Buy your favorite chocolates and dress them up.*

MATERIALS

chocolate buttons or tablets (available at cooking stores or candymaking section of craft supply stores)

cranberry luster dust, green pearl dust (white dust with a slight greenish hue) (see p. 76 for references.)

candy mold

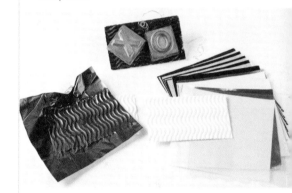

corrugated paper

plastic coated silver wire

foil candy wrappers

plastic treat bags

scissors or craft knife

new paintbrush (dedicated to candy decorating)

double boiler or microwave

thin vinyl or latex kitchen gloves

7. Brush luster dust on chocolates.

8. Put chocolates in wrappers and fold top edge to back; close with twists of wire, or seal with a sticker.

TIP *Use a mix of dark chocolate and milk chocolate. The soft, round flavor of the milk chocolate will make it palatable for most people, but the toasty, forceful flavor of the dark chocolate adds a depth that assures the favor won't be a cutesy candy but, rather, an elegant treat.*

VARIATION

Particularly fun for kids are chocolate pops. What is it about food on a stick that appeals to the child in us—not to mention actual children? Who knows, but it is a hit with the youngsters. Pick up some paper lollipop sticks at your candymaking source to transform chocolates into pops.

Ring around the finger

ROUND SCRUBBY SOAP

MATERIALS

clear glycerin

soap glitter (we used a blend of gold and red)

soap fragrance

soap mold

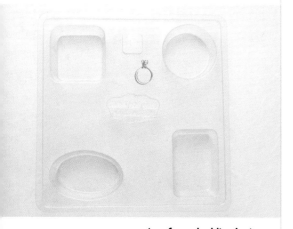

rings for embedding (twist your own out of craft wire or buy toy rings or faux wedding ring decorations)

round wood or paper box

clear bags or plastic wrap

wire

decorative paper

glue stick

scissors or craft knife

double boiler or microwave

measuring cup

Come clean. Please. These sudsy favors are a gift for the home of friends and family. They are also a whimsical reference to starting with a clean slate and a new beginning. It's easy to incorporate a theme, such as a decorative element you are using elsewhere (like fish, the sign of good luck in many cultures). Or, you can give a matrimonial wink and embed toy rings in the soap that recall the new ones on your finger.

DIRECTIONS

1. Melt chunks of clear glycerin in double boiler or microwave (follow directions on package). Note the capacity of your mold and use a bit more than you will need to fill the molds.

2. Add a one pinch of glitter per soap, 3 to 6 fragrance drops. Refrain from stirring; swirl the soap gently so as not to create too many bubbles or froth.

3. Pour melted soap in measuring cup, then into mold cavities. Stop halfway through the pour and place the rings in the mold. Finish pouring the melted soap into the mold (gently, so as not to disturb the rings).

4. Tap mold to get rid of air bubbles. Let cool completely (1 to 2 hours) then pop out of the mold.

5. For packaging, wrap soap in plastic. Use a glue stick to cover a round box with very sheer decorative paper; let the paper drape naturally then smooth it down. Wrap some wire around the box and twist the ends in a "knot."

VARIATIONS

Make the soaps colorful. Add just a few drops of colorant and the misty translucency of the glycerin soap will remain. Mold them into a variety of shapes.

TIP *Always wrap glycerin soap in plastic first because it is very soft and will smear.*

Anniversary Bonsai
MINIATURE TREE STARTER KIT

Bonsai are miniature trees trimmed and cultivated in small pots to grow in interesting shapes and in miniature form. They require care and can live for a very long time. Visit some botanical gardens that have a bonsai section and you will see some well over one hundred years old. Give guests a starter kit (that is mess free, to boot). The long-growing gift is a symbol of longevity and care.

DIRECTIONS

1. Cut a piece of decorative paper to wrap around the box, and glue it to the exterior.

2. Nestle peat pellet in bonsai pot and place it in box; pack moss around pot.

3. To make miniseed pack: Cut a small rectangle of paper and fold into thirds. Fold one end over middle third, and glue long edges together. Fold other end over and trim to create envelope flap. Place three to five seeds inside. Make a "seeds" label on a piece of contrasting paper and glue it to the front of the pack.

4. To make directions to include: Fold a piece of paper in half. Trace circular object so that side of circle aligns with folded edge. Cut around traced line, leaving the folded edge that aligns with the side of the circle. You now have a circular card in which to include instructions. Include the following points in the instructions: "To use peat pellet, first moisten in pot; then place one or two seeds in peat; keep moist. When the plant outgrows pot, transplant into a larger pot or outdoors."

5. Make name tag out of coordinating paper and punch $1/8$" (0.3 cm) hole in one end. You can also include the name of the tree seeds on the tag.

6. Place directions and seeds inside box and close.

7. Wrap floral wire around box and twist tightly at top; thread name tag on wire; curl ends of wire around pencil.

NOTE *Sizes will be determined by the pot you choose.*

miniature bonsai pots or other small ceramic pots

tree seeds

dry peat pellets (for seed starting)

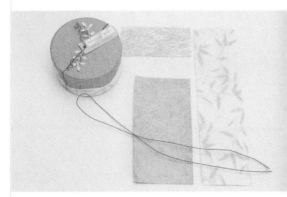

kraft paper boxes

moss

cloth-covered floral wire

assorted papers

pencil or pen

glue stick

scissors or craft knife

$1/8$" (0.3 cm) hole punch (optional)

Forever Etched in Memory
FROSTED GLASSWARE

MATERIALS

glasses

coordinating beads

silver-colored wire,
20 gauge and 34 gauge

adhesive vinyl

Etchall glass etching
crème

small paintbrush

hole punches (We used
star $1/4$" (0.5cm),
$1/8$" (0.3 cm) circle,
and a crescent)

round-nosed pliers

rubber gloves

metal-rimmed
vellum tags

fine point pen

Gone are the typical frosted wine and champagne glasses. We like the idea, though, of etched glasses. The permanence of glass etched with a design transforms the ordinary into intriguing. What better occasion to toast to the future than a wedding celebration? Lift these colorful cordial glasses in honor of the happy couple (or in honor of the attending guests as any good host would do) and the etching takes on a different tone. Rather than proper and fussy, these glasses look useful and well crafted, in the vein of the everyday art of the Arts and Crafts movement.

TIP *Cut the vinyl into small pieces when working on a curved surface so that it doesn't wrinkle.*

(fig. 1)

DIRECTIONS

ETCH THE GLASS

1. Punch a design into the adhesive vinyl (*see fig. 1*). Punches come in various designs, so you can personalize the design very easily and quickly.

2. Wash and dry the glass with a lint-free rag. Try not to get any fingerprints on the areas of the glass to be etched.

3. Apply the vinyl pattern to the glass and press it firmly in place.

4. Following the manufacturer's directions, apply a thick even layer of crème to the glass using a small brush. Wait 5 minutes, then rinse the glass off under warm running water and remove the vinyl pattern. Be sure to wear rubber gloves when working with etching crème.

MAKE THE WIRE NAME TAGS

1. Cut off about 6" (15 cm) of 20 gauge wire and about 7" (18 cm) of 34 gauge wire. Begin wrapping the 34 gauge loosely around the 20 gauge.

2. Slip the name tag and bead on the wire. Be sure to select a bead that has a large enough hole to fit around the wire.

3. Curl one end of the wire around a few times using round-nosed pliers, and press the spiral up to keep the bead and tag in place (*see fig. 2*). To create the name tag that fits over the edge of a glass, simply bend it over the edge of the glass and press in place; then curl the other end into a spiral to finish. To create a tag that fits around the base of the glass, follow the instructions above but wrap it around the base of the glass rather than over the edge. To finish, bend the wire to make a hook for closing.

(fig. 2)

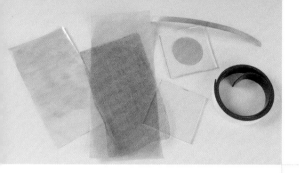

Reflections of Love

MINIMIRROR FAVOR

MATERIALS

Krylon's Looking Glass
Base Coat Mirror Paint
and Clear Coat Sealer
or other spray-mirror
product

newspaper (to protect
work surface from
spray paint)

small squares of glass
(approximately 2" × 2"
(5 cm × 5 cm)

template from page 72

blue vellum and
paper cutouts

glue stick

circular stickers or shelf
lining paper cut into
shapes (for masking)

silvered copper tape

self-adhesive
magnetic strips

Many favors are comestible. Guests eat chocolates, cakes, and candies as they drive home after the festivities, for breakfast the next morning when they wake up late, or for a midnight snack. Some favors do away with food in exchange for a little art. This keepsake favor is a little unusual because it recalls the wedding but without the need for names and dates. A further deviation from the norm is the unique construction of the project—the mirror finish is sprayed on. Carefully lifting a heart shape (or floral shape) from the mirror makes a unique reminder of the event.

DIRECTIONS

1. Cut out templates from adhesive paper, using the shapes from page 72, or create your own. Clean the surface of the glass squares very well and apply adhesive templates onto the glass.

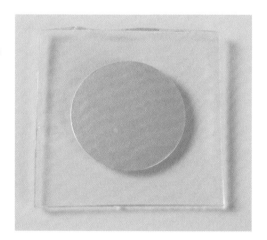

TIP *Mirror spray takes a little finesse to work with. Experiment a few times before committing yourself to the project. Make sure the glass is very clean and peel the stencils off carefully.*

(fig. 1)

2. Place the prepared glass on newsprint with the stencils facing up. Working in a well-ventilated area, coat the glass with several thin layers of mirror paint and let dry 15 minutes. Coat the painted surface with the sealer following the product instructions and carefully remove the stencil. Let dry. *(see fig. 1)*

3. Turn over the glass so the mirrored area shows through from the back. Cut vellum to size and affix a paper motif to its center. Sandwich the paper between two pieces of glass so that the motif shows through the clear area of the mirrored glass. *(see fig. 2)*

4. Seal the edges of the glass with silvered copper tape and affix thin magnetic strips to the back.

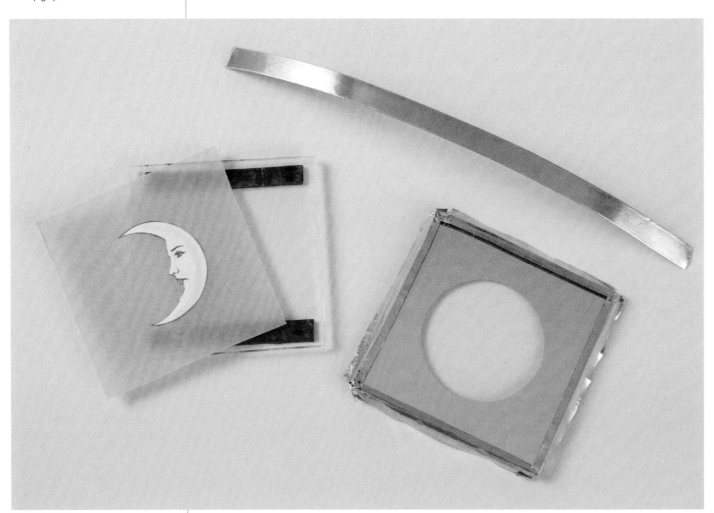

(fig. 2)

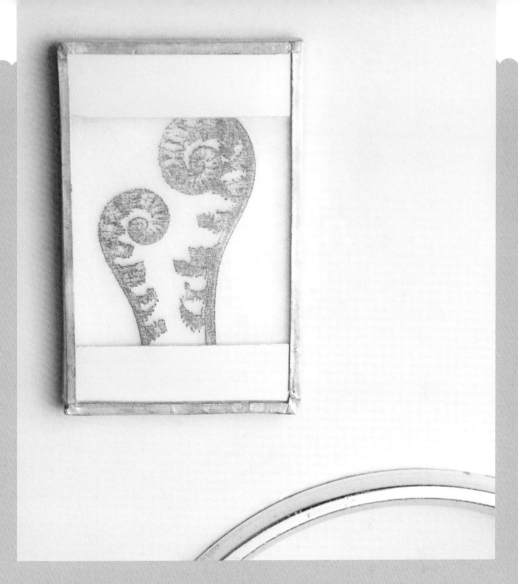

VARIATIONS

• Sandwich a photocopy on acetate between the mirrored glass (we used an image of two ferns). For a diffused effect, gently abrade the back of the acetate with steel wool before inserting the image.

• You can use a different shape if hearts are too standard for you. Go floral with a rounded petal shape or block off a word with stickers for a mirror that really says something.

• Krylon also makes a frosted spray, so you can mirror an entire piece of glass and use a stencil on the front side of the glass to block off a frosted image.

Henna Party
MENDHI KIT

All over the world, women decorate themselves as part of the wedding ritual. Your most familiar form of decoration might be a veil and an up-do—or a manicure. Mendhi application on hands and feet is a common wedding preparation in India. It uses the same process as a henna tattoo that you might see available in some salons and stores—the henna is a plant derivative that temporarily dyes the skin for up to a few weeks. The traditional patterns are lovely and intricate. This kit is the perfect reference to wedding traditions and is also thoroughly modern. Make the kit as a favor for a wedding shower. But, because the dye lasts for a few weeks, make sure that no one in the wedding ceremony uses the kit without knowing fully that it will last. If you are inspired by the henna idea and want to incorporate that tradition into your wedding, visit a professional salon that routinely applies Mendhi patterns and go to your wedding with a little more tradition and filigree.

DIRECTIONS

1. Cut the cardboard into a square measuring 10" × 10" (25 cm × 25 cm) and score two lines down the center of the square to create a "spine." Cut the yellow card stock to fit inside the cardboard "book" and glue with PVA.

2. Layer two rectangles of hand-made paper on top of the yellow card stock. Cut a rectangle of yellow card stock and glue to the front cover. Layer with origami mesh paper and a paisley design cut from vellum. (See the template on page 30 or use clip art.)

3. Place vellum on top of the templates (see pages 72–73) and trace the Mendhi patterns. Fill three glassine envelopes with henna, tea, and some Mendhi designs.

4. Create a small booklet from card stock and vellum in which you explain the process of applying henna designs. Affix all four pieces with clear photo corners to the inside of the kit.

MATERIALS

henna

loose tea

templates from
pages 72–73

decorative cardboard

yellow ochre card stock

rice paper, origami mesh
and vellum

glassine envelopes

clear photo corners

glue stick

craft glue

scissors

craft knife and
cutting mat

felt tipped pen

raffia

circular tags

string

PVA adhesive

See page 72-73 for these templates

MEHNDI DIRECTIONS TO INCLUDE IN KIT

1. Brew the tea and add to the henna powder until it forms a mudlike paste. Add lemon juice and olive oil and let sit for at least 1 hour (overnight is best).

2. Wash skin and apply the henna paste with a fine stick (such as a toothpick) making sure only a thin line of henna touches the skin, not the end of the stick.

3. Let dry several hours and apply lemon juice to moisten the henna as it sets. When the henna has turned a deep red color, carefully scrape off the paste, rub the skin with olive oil, and rinse the area with water. Avoid using soap to prolong the design, which will last for about 2 weeks.

4. For design inspiration, see *Traditional Mehndi Designs: A Treasury of Henna Body Art* by Dorine van den Beukel.

First Impressions

METALLIC CLAY TILE FRAME

MATERIALS

paperclay (or self-drying clay)

basswood for frame (or an unfinished wood frame)

spackle

acrylic paints

metallic wax (We used silver Rub 'n Buff Wax.)

craft glue (such as Sobo or Tacky Glue)

glass

brushes

craft knife

rolling pin (or cylindrical bottle)

sandpaper

objects to imprint in clay

cardboard, cut to the same size as the frame.

Friends are great collaborators—when you're up to no good (Who skipped college classes with you in favor of a road trip to Niagara Falls?)—and when you want to make something nice. This project calls on everyone's innate ability to read into symbols and make something while talking and laughing. It's a great shower project, so show it to the party organizer . . . or make it at the next night-in with the group. Each of your friends at the party can be in charge of a tile, bringing with them an object that signifies some aspect of marriage, or a memoir of your relationship with your sweetheart. The object does not need to be literal, and only you and your friends might know what the imprint of your cell phone means. This project will not interrupt the talking and frolicking.

DIRECTIONS

1. Build a frame from basswood (or use an unfinished wood frame) and coat it with spackle. Let dry and sand smooth before staining with diluted acrylic paints *(see fig. 1)*. (The spackle gives the effect of grout when the tiles are applied on top.

2. Measure your frame to decide the dimensions of the tiles. Flatten the paperclay with a rolling pin to desired thickness and cut with a craft knife to create tiles *(see fig. 2)*.

3. Press found objects into the clay, smooth the edges, and let dry.

4. Paint the tiles with acrylics and let dry. Then rub metallic wax on the tiles to create an aged effect *(see fig. 3)*.

5. Glue the tiles to the frame and let dry. Insert glass, photo, and cardboard backing into the finished frame.

(fig. 1)

(fig. 2)

(fig. 3)

Sleeping Beauties

SILKY SLEEP MASK

We all know that planning a wedding can take a lot of energy (although, we sincerely hope that you don't overtax yourself). Even the smallest exertion can rightfully require a renewed habit of napping. We think it's a good idea: Keep your mood high, your energy at top peak, and your skin glowing (extra sleep really does help). Mellow out in style with these silk eye masks. Make a set for your entire bridal party. Better yet, make them at a shower or get-together—each person can make one for someone else. And don't forget the gents. They can use a little snazzy shut-eye as well. Maybe without flowers—or maybe with them.

MATERIALS

dupione silk

silk flowers

flax seed

silk ribbon

fabric glue

scissors

wire cutters

needle and thread

DIRECTIONS

1. Cut out two rectangles of dupione silk measuring approximately 4" × 11" (10 cm × 28 cm). With the silk's right side facing up, apply fabric glue to three edges of one of the rectangles. Place the right side of the second rectangle on top and press the glued seams with your fingers.

2. Trim silk flowers from their stems with wire cutters. After the glue on the rectangle's seams is dry, turn the fabric right side out. Arrange the petals on the silk, affix with a dot of fabric glue and let dry.

3. Use a running stitch to sew a ribbon on each end of the rectangle. Fill the open end of the mask with flax seed and seal the end seam with more fabric glue.

VARIATION

Use loose silk petals trapped under netting instead of gluing the flowers in a specific pattern.

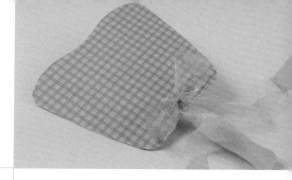

Portable Breeze

COLORFUL FAN

Summer is a popular wedding season. That means blue skies, gorgeous flowers, and heat. The stagnant air that we blissfully pretend to ignore can transform the most well-turned-out wedding guest into a puddle before the vows are even uttered—especially if the wedding is outdoors. Arm guests with a little air-conditioning and fill the gathering with a uniform color. It's dual purposed: coolant and decoration. Imagine a field of friends, fluttering vibrant hand-printed paper—a field of happy, cool people.

DIRECTIONS

1. Enlarge and trace the template on page 74 onto the card stock and the decorative paper. Cut out two shapes from the card stock and one shape from the decorative paper.

2. Apply hot-melt glue to half of the handle and press firmly onto one card stock cut-out, making sure it is centered.

3. Spray the decorative paper with spray adhesive, in a well-ventilated area (or outdoors). Line up the decorative paper with the second card stock cut-out and press firmly together, pressing out all the air bubbles.

4. Use spray adhesive to join the two halves of the fan together. Line up the edges carefully. The decorative paper should face out (obviously), and the handle should be sandwiched between fan layers. Press firmly to assure a good contact between the paper.

5. Trim any uneven edges. Punch a small hole on each side of the handle at the base of the fan. Thread the ribbon through and tie.

TIP *If an outdoor wedding is in your plans, remind people on the invitation to wear a hat. Not only are hats a marvelous wedding standard, they will protect people from the harsh sun.*

MATERIALS

card stock paper

template from page 74

coordinating decorative paper

tongue depressors, or specially made balsa handles from the craft store

hot-melt glue gun

spray mount

scissors

¼" (0.5cm) holepunch

ribbon

VARIATION

You can run the card stock through the printer before you cut out the shield shape. Print your names and the date or a quote or image.

VARIATION

The shield shape seems to catch the air very well, but other shapes are suitable, too. Circles can look neat (and are easy to cut out with a compass cutter). You can even scan in a leaf into your computer, lighten the color, print it out onto light green paper and make leaf fans for everyone.

Swirly Container

INTERLOCKING PETAL BOX

MATERIALS

card stock paper

template from page 74

decorative paper

scissors

pencil

spray adhesive

straight edge

bone folder

4" (10 cm) circle of tulle

ribbon

wildflower seeds or
lavender flowers

color printer

VARIATION

*Consider filling the box
with rose petals to be
tossed as confetti during
the evening, or with
candy-coated chocolate,
without the need for
a tuille bag. Instead of
making your own tuille
gather, you could purchase
premade tuille bags in
many different colors at
craft stores.*

These little boxes were inspired by a chocolate that arrived in a
similar, but stouter, box. The chocolate was good, but the box
was fabulous. The interlocking tabs are petal-like, making the
box a perfect container for wildflower seeds. Of course, the
boxes could hold candied almonds, sweets, rose petals, or any
number of other things.

DIRECTIONS

1. Using the template on page 74, trace the box shape onto card stock paper and decorative
   paper. Cut out the shapes.

2. Use spray adhesive to glue the card stock and decorative paper shapes together. Take care
   to line up the shapes and have "right sides" facing outward (there usually is no right side
   to card stock, though). Press firmly and use the edge of a bone folder to force out any
   air bubbles.

3. Line up the straight edge along the fold lines and score the line with the tip of the bone
   folder. Fold the flaps of the box up along the score lines.

4. Prepare the box contents. You can put candies or petals directly in the box. Or, gather
   candies or wildflower seeds in a circle of tuille and tie the small bundle closed with a
   ribbon. Put the bundle inside the box and interlock the swirly flaps to close the box.

TIP *If printing out a message that lines up with the bottom of the box is too much hassle, print a sheet of
"bottoms," cut them out, and glue them into the box bottoms.*

Wintery Topiary

BEADED PLACE CARD HOLDER

Place cards can range anywhere from a simple piece of paper to a river pebble with a name written across it to a portable *objet d'art*. This place card adds some glamour to the glimmering lights. Crown each place setting with a beaded topiary and guests will know where they sit in style. The small tree will shimmer in the candlelight as the white and teal beads catch the light. The colors are particularly appropriate for a winter wedding.

DIRECTIONS

1. Paint the terra-cotta pot, dowel, and Styrofoam ball in a color that coordinates with your table setting (we used various shades of turquoise with silvery metallics) and set aside to dry. Rub metallic wax over the painted pot and burnish with a soft cloth.

2. Insert florist's foam into the pot and then glue a circle of decorative paper to the top of the foam. Leaving 1" (3 cm) bare on each end of the dowel, brush it with craft glue and wind with strung beads.

3. Brush the top 1" (3 cm) of the beaded "stem" with glue and push into the Styrofoam ball. Apply craft glue to the painted ball and sprinkle with micro beads. Push the topiary into the florist's foam and allow to dry.

4. Embellish the pot with organza ribbon and a vellum place card.

MATERIALS

styrofoam ball

small terra-cotta pot

thin dowel (for stem)

florist's foam

strung beads

micro beads

metallic paper

organza ribbon

craft glue

acrylic paints

metallic wax (We used Rub 'n Buff.)

cloth or fine steel wool

vellum

wire

bay leaves

paper fern leaves (at a paper or craft store)

styrofoam ball

twig

small terra-cotta pot

moss

florist's foam

ribbon

card stock

alphabet stamps and ink pad

acrylic paints

hot-melt glue gun

sandpaper

bronze gel pen

VARIATION

You can also evoke the Tuscan hillsides, aromatic food, and wonderful glasses of Montepulciano. The relaxed, sun-soaked feeling of this terra-cotta version will enhance any robust, festive, and rustic reception. Depending on the materials used, guests may enjoy a lingering scent of the hills outside of Florence for weeks to come.

DIRECTIONS

1. Cut a twig to the appropriate length for your topiary and poke a hole in the base of a Styrofoam ball. Hot glue bay leaves and paper ferns to the ball and set aside.

2. Paint the twig with metallic acrylic paint and inject hot glue into the hole at the ball's base.

3. Paint the terra-cotta pot with antique white acrylic paint, let dry, and sand to distress the finish.

4. Push florist's foam into the pot and glue the twig and ball structure into the foam. Finish with a layer of moss, wire ribbon, and a name tag with hand-stamped letters.

PLACE CARD IDEAS

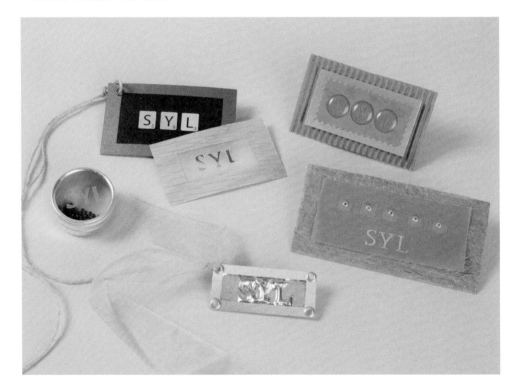

Sign in Here

MATERIALS

blank "memory" books

decorative papers:
blue and white vellum,
blue and white Japanese
lace paper

white tulle

antique, lowercase
alphabet stamp set

black ink pad
(to coordinate with
black wire binding)

scissors or craft knife

glue stick

colored pencils and
other art supplies

scallop paper edgers
(optional)

It is kind of silly for guests to stand in line as they enter a reception, waiting to sign their names in the small space allotted in the guest book. Or should guests remember to leave their dinner companions and sign the book, midparty? Aren't we all tempted to take up more than a single line, anyway? Give each table a couple of miniature guest books instead. Guests can write, draw, and share their stories about the bride and groom in each book, bride stories in "she" and groom tales in "he." After the event, the bride and groom can read all the books and share all their great stories (that they might not have shared yet). Enhance the creativity quotient and stash pens, pencils, crayons, and Polaroid iZone cameras with sticky film on each table.

DIRECTIONS

1. Stamp "he" on lower right corner of a book and "she" on the other. Let dry. Ink on vellum takes longer to dry than it does on regular paper.

2. Place a square of blue vellum over the "he" stamping, then top with a smaller square of blue lace paper. Place a piece of tulle over the "she" stamping and top with a smaller square of white lace paper. Use a glue stick and small dabs in the corners of the materials to secure; any more will be too much for thin, delicate papers and fabric, and would cause the vellum to wrinkle.

3. Bundle pencils together and wrap with a piece of vellum. Use glue to seal. We trimmed the vellum with scallop paper edgers.

DIRECTIONS

1. Stamp "he" on lower right corner of a book and "she" on the other. Let dry. Ink on vellum takes longer to dry than it does on regular paper.

2. Place a square of blue vellum over the "he" stamping, then top with a smaller square of blue lace paper. Place a piece of tulle over the "she" stamping and top with a smaller square of white lace paper. Use a glue stick and small dabs in the corners of the materials to secure; any more will be too much for thin, delicate papers and fabric, and would cause the vellum to wrinkle.

3. Bundle pencils together and wrap with a piece of vellum. Use glue to seal. We trimmed the vellum with scallop paper edgers.

VARIATION

A larger book means more room to draw. Stamp "guests" on a piece of torn paper and layer it over handmade paper. Add a fiber border and a fiber place marker. Cover a can with decorative paper and tie with a fiber that matches the book's place marker. Fill the can with writing supplies.

Underwater Hurricane

SWIRLY BLUE CANDLEHOLDERS

MATERIALS

Mod Podge
(or decoupage medium
or collage glue)

foam brush

tissue paper

stamps (We used
Stampendous! Perfectly
Clear Stamps; the set is
called Maggie's Daisy and
includes both stamps;
product number SSC002.)

stamp ink pad (We used a
Kaleidacolor Raised
Rainbow Dye Inkpad
by Tsukineko; the
color scheme is "Blue
Breeze" and there are
five color variations.)

glass vase and votives

Candlelight does wonders for ambiance. The flicker of candles adds a fire and sparkle to both eyes and moods, and everyone looks phenomenal with the soft, ever-changing light. Enhance that trend by decorating tables with these large lanterns and miniature votives. Each table will be swimming in a shimmering blue, a mix of campfire, romantic dinner, and the deep sky.

VARIATION

Consider a warm alternate to the color palette: Cover rounded glass votives with tangerine-colored tissue. Use delicate dried flowers as a substitute for stamped design accents. In our version, we created a slightly darker background for the flower using a more intense shade of tissue. After the tissue layer is completely dry, add a drop of glue, then gently press the flower onto the surface and smooth it out. Once that dries, coat the entire flower with a layer of Mod Podge or other decoupage medium to protect it.

(fig. 1)

1. Use a ruler to tear tissue into strips of different widths; trap the tissue underneath the ruler, and pull up on one side. This will give you a straight, even tear *(see fig. 1)*.

2. Brush Mod Podge on the vase or on a votive; lay a strip of tissue on top, making sure it is fairly straight. Smooth the strip down with the brush; use additional Mod Podge if neces sary. Continue layering strips until you are happy with the level of transparency (three lay ers works well). **N O T E :** Strips do not have to be perfectly sized before applying them; you can tear off the top and bottom once the Mod Podge has set—then you will have a bit of an edge to smooth over the top and bottom edges of the glass.

(fig. 2)

3. Stamp some strips with the flower motif. When dry, adhere to the vase and votives.
   N O T E : The stamp pad we used goes from light to dark blue; so for some of the flower stamping we used two or three different colors at once. For the smaller stamp we used one color per stamping *(see fig. 2)*.

4. Stamp the swirl directly on the vases and votives when the Mod Podge is dry.

Flowers for Everyone

MATERIALS

4 square vases

green bamboo

white waterlilly dahlia

river stones

water

sharp knife

Flower styling is more of an art than a craft. You need to see the end result in your head before starting and sculpt the arrangement into being as you go. If you've got the hang of it, flower arranging can be a great and innovative way to add your spark to the surroundings (besides with your dazzling self). It is fairly common to see large bundles of flowers in pinks, purples, and whites do duty as a table centerpiece. Because you've already seen that a million times, we feel you can probably pull it off already. We want to show you some different paths that an arrangement can take.

Flowers are also a great way to bridge the sometimes formidable distance between traditional and supermodern. Really, that distance is not so great—so many of us have facets in both domains. Those traits, attitudes, and tendencies combine well into a personality, but still, it can be difficult to put that same balance into action in a big event, when you need it the most. A bundle of traditional flowers (favorites through the ages) can soften the hard lines and colors of a modern setting, whether it's the modern architecture of a church, or your grandparents' Frank Lloyd Wright Usonian. By the same token, sleek, elegant

1. Cut the bamboo into equal lengths that just fit into the square vases, lying down.

2. Fill each vase differently. One vase can be filled entirely with bamboo. Another can be partially filled with bamboo and topped with a single white flower. Others can include river stones and any other simple combination of basic materials.

flower arrangements that rely on strong lines and shape will do wonders to modernize the historic home that the reception is set in. We are not suggesting that you use modern flower arrangements to mask the filigreed crown molding. If you try to do that, the design elements will not build on each other but, rather, look unpaired. With the right balance of styles, you can enhance both the traditional and contemporary. Do a little experimentation along the lines of *Homefront in the Garden* (from the BBC) and apply their concept of supermodern meets ordinary flowers, because it can work vice-versa as well. We are even particularly fond of a haphazard bundle of wildflowers in a watering can if the setting is right.

Typically, a bride has a bouquet (but not always—you could just carry a purse, or nothing at all), the groom has a boutonniere, the wedding party has their respective flowers, and then there are decorative flowers for the wedding and reception sites. Take a swatch of the dress fabric to the florist and match some of the flowers for the boutonniere to that color. Do so even if it's a white dress, because there are so many varieties of white; it could be anything from snow, eggshell, pearl, glacier, bone, or even cloud—some are more yellow than others and you don't want a flower to make the dress look dingy. Even if none of the other flowers match a certain color scheme, the two of you will "match" if the boutonniere coordinates with the dress.

For the reception space, keep in mind that a table's centerpiece rests between one guest trying to have a conversation with another on the opposite side of the table. A gorgeous 3-foot (91 cm)-tall bundle of assorted garden delights can be a serious hindrance to an otherwise brilliant conversation if people cannot maintain eye contact without getting a kink in the neck. The solution may be small vases. Sure, on a table that seats eight people, a 4-inch (10 cm)-tall vase can look dinky. It won't look undersized at all, though, if you use four of them together as a single centerpiece. These square vases hold chopped bamboo in a most unusual way—more as terrain than cut flower. Arranging each square of the centerpiece in a slightly different way adds texture and variety to the table and allows people a field of garden goodness without the need to peer through foliage.

VARIATION

Is it the vase or the champagne that makes things teeter? Roly vases are part decoration and part game. Create a triad of gerbera daisies in the middle of the table and watch guests play with the vases.

VARIATION

Height doesn't have to be an enemy. A moderately tall vase is easy to manage. And simple arrangements of a single type of flower are the easiest for you to pull off. Bundle a thick handful of calla lilies, holding them in place with clear hair elastics. Trim the bottoms so they are flat and even. Rest the bottoms of the calla lilies on the table and ease the bundle off to the side, titling the bundle with the bottoms still resting on the table. The stems remain parallel to each other but each flower is visible in a kind of upright cascade. Cut the bottoms even to the right length and stand in a thin vase.

Diversions Add Texture

AN OCCUPIED GUEST IS A HAPPY GUEST

Hosting a wedding comprises a lot of little things. A meaningful ceremony paired with a party sounds simple enough, and it can be, but some elements can transform a good host into a great one. Try throwing an event that matches your style and personality and puts the guests at ease, whether it's a barbeque or a black tie affair. The other is

providing guests with a balance of activities that allows them to look after themselves. After all, you can't watch over them at every moment of the day.

The surest way to keep guests active and happy, without additional attention, is to creatively mix guests together. You are hip and fascinating, and chances are a good percentage of your guests are, too. The wallflowers are fascinating, too, and they will get drawn into conversations by your friends with an ample supply of aplomb. Planning seating arrangements can be taxing, but getting together a mix of potential conversationalists is part of the fun. (Katie is a chemist, and so is Michael. Michael's wife is studying to be a master sommelier, and Jared loves to eat out—perfect!). People of the same age do not automatically have common interests, so consider personality more than generational guides. Young and old may like the same things and have an amazing time together. Don't let age be the stringent rule for seating.

But aside from riveting conversation, what more can be done to keep people happy? There is dinner, which in our circles always keeps the conversation going and going and going. There is also dancing, which keeps a party roaring. But not all activity needs to be major. Sometimes, the small filler bits provide enough play to help transition between activities and keep the party moving. What to do when there is a lull in the conversation, or when the photos have gone on forty minutes longer than planned, or when dancers need a break and sit back down at a semiempty table? Provide "fidget toys." Those are items that don't take a lot of concentration but provide a minute or two of diversion while striking up a new conversation. Things like pinball boxes with ball-bearings, spinning tops that coordinate with the décor, fortune-tellers (remember those folded-paper toys?) that are filled with romantic questions or "predictions."

Some weddings are a reunion of far-flung friends and family that have shared your world-wide adventures. It is possible that there will be tables where few people know each other. Help them find conversation by including a little icebreaker. Include a list of adventures that you have shared with people at the table as a way to make their introductions easier. The person the groom backpacked across Norway with might not introduce himself that way, so a little hint ensures that the conversation kicks off to a great start. If there are only a few tables filled with strangers, you have a choice as good hosts: rush to those tables first to make effusive introductions or, better yet, arm some of the outgoing friends at each table with a little history beforehand. That way, the conversation will start with "So, Alice tells me you're an astronaut," or "What was it like cooking for the president of France?" It will take off from there.

If the event is complicated (and even some easy-to-put-together ones are), you can print up programs for each place setting. If dancing is a major part of your vision, you can hint for guests to hit the dance floor with a program decorated with dance-step instructions.

Whatever the situation, if you supply guests with their basic needs for enjoyment—food, drink, and conversation—they will pretty much take care of themselves, leaving you time to visit with as many people as possible and enjoy the kick-off to your marriage instead of worrying about whether people are having fun or not.

Wishing Tree

We like the idea of fêting a couple and their new marriage with everyone's best wishes. Sure, we wish people well all the time, but this occasion calls for a little extra demonstration of our hopes for their future. Set a collection of curly willow branches somewhere at the reception next to a stack of vellum leaves and a pen. People will take the time to write a short message to the couple, a wish for their future, or a piece of wisdom they want to share. As the evening progresses, the tree will fill with leaves that flutter as people walk or dance by.

DIRECTIONS

1. Place vellum on top of the templates and trace leaf shapes (or invent your own). Cut out the leaves and punch a ¼" (0.5 cm) -hole at the base of each. Insert an eyelet in each hole and affix with an eyelet tool and hammer.

2. Thread 4" (10 cm) of fine wire through each eyelet and twist to secure.

3. Push curly willow into florist's foam, insert in a planter, and layer moss on top of the foam. Tie three layers of organdy ribbon around the planter (or use dyed raffia for a more rustic effect). Have the leaves and metallic pens ready next to the wish tree for guests to write on as they arrive. Attach the leaves to the branches with the wire.

MATERIALS

curly willow

vellum

planter

ribbon

hole punch (We used ¼" (0.5 cm))

eyelets and eyelet tool

florist's wire

florist's foam

dried moss

metallic gel pens

wire cutters

scissors

leaf images templates (see page 75)

Fortune Cache

MATERIALS

matchboxes

assorted handmade
papers

charms

beads (for "feet" on
bottom of boxes)

Sobo craft glue

E6000 silicone glue (for
attaching charms and
beads)

gel pen

embroidery thread

Opening things gives everyone a thrill. It doesn't matter what it is, we love to reveal the hidden goodies. The joy of it never leaves us—that's the key to exciting gifts and direct-mail offers. Guests sit down to this miniature chest made from a decoupaged matchbox that is set on a platform of wire and beads. No one but the most fatigued or disenchanted could resist opening it up to see what is inside. Place a little fortune or well-wishes inside to reward their eternal and sprightly curiosity. The treasure could be a message from you and your sweetheart, a pebble with a word on it, or a small, emblematic object for them to keep in their pockets.

DIRECTIONS

1. Cut papers to the appropriate sizes for the matchbox's drawer and exterior.

2. Glue papers on the outside and inside of the box. Create a miniature collage on the top of the box by combining a variety of paper textures, patterns, and colors.

3. Attach a charm on top of the collage with the silicone glue and let set. Adhere the bead "feet" in the same manner on the bottom of the box.

4. Write a quote or a fortune for your guest on a piece of the handmade paper, roll up into a scroll, and wrap with embroidery thread. Place the secret message inside the box.

TIP *Consider including a favorite poem rolled on a scroll of paper, a small seashell or keepsake from a recent trip, a pressed leaf, seeds for a plant that you love, or a list of other historic occasions that occurred on the same date as your wedding.*

Kids are Guests, Too

HOW TO ENTERTAIN YOUR SMALL CELEBRANTS

We're firm believers that it's OK to be a kid. So often kids are placed in situations where they have to act grown-up, sit still, and be quiet. That doesn't seem so fair when they haven't developed the skills that let them do that for hours on end. (Frankly, there are adults that haven't developed that skill either.) If you are including the kids on your guest list, be kind to them and give them some tools to have an enjoyable day, too.

The smallest children really want attention. And at a wedding there are often plenty of adults and family members that are happy to cuddle and hold the young niece they hardly ever see. The older children are, however, the more they need something beyond time sitting on Aunt Florence's lap.

BOREDOM IS THE ENEMY

Parents of unhappy kids are unhappy guests. They feel tired and annoyed and unable to fully enjoy the celebration. But kids shouldn't be made to sit on their hands just to keep their parents happy. That's unrealistic and not that nice. Instead, remember that the reception is a party for everyone, young and old, and give the younger set the chance to revel in their vices as well (OK, playing with toys and eating candy doesn't yet qualify as a vice, but you get our meaning).

FOOD

Many an otherwise happy kid was rendered miserable by elaborate food that is overwhelming to their palates. Discuss food options ahead of time with parents if you're concerned. Arrange a tray of PB&Js, chips, and other standard goodies that kids can retreat to if they can't handle the farfalle with foie gras and truffle oil . . . or the chicken. Even if they've cried "finished!" after three bites of the grown-up meal, they may get peckish again before the party's over. Keeping kid-friendly food handy is never a mistake.

THE "HARD STUFF"

Many parents try to keep the kids away from sweets, but the adults are living it up, and the kids should be allowed to, too. Dole out the sweets in a fun way. Create a tray with small bundles of goodies. The small packages will mitigate the tummyaches (maybe) and allow kids to have a container all to themselves. Wrap three licorice ropes with a fourth for a sweet bundle. Make small "bags" out of colorful paper and fill with small candies like M&Ms or miniature candy bars.

PLAYTIME

Kids will run around, dance up a storm, and play with other young guests. But if there won't be more than a couple kids, offer up some play materials to keep the young set happy and entertained. Cars and trucks are perfect tabletop entertainment for boys and girls. Driving a fire truck along the table can keep a child enthralled in make-believe land for a while. And what more perfect kid-themed favor than a new toy? For those in prime dress-up age, you can include some hats like old ladies wore to tea ages ago, tiaras, cowboy hats, or sheriff badges. You don't want to turn the reception into a circus, but two or three kids running around hardly makes a circus. Or save the dress-up goods for a relaxed rehearsal dinner.

Never underestimate the power of crayons, colored pencils, and paper to amuse kids and keep them in high spirits (forget about the markers . . . you don't want them around dress-up clothes).

WHERE TO PUT IT ALL

You don't want the kids' diversions to dominate or distract others, but a little planning will keep kids and their parents in the mood to celebrate. All you need is a small collection of objects and goodies appropriate for the size of the gathering and the number of kids. You can arrange a small table with the munchies off to the side. The toys can be given directly to the parents for dispensing when the kids get a little antsy.

When you are having a party, you are host to all guests, big and little. A little attention to these smaller participants may not fix all the fussing, but the effort expended is worth it.

Templates

Henna Party templates, page 28

Reflection of Love template, page 24

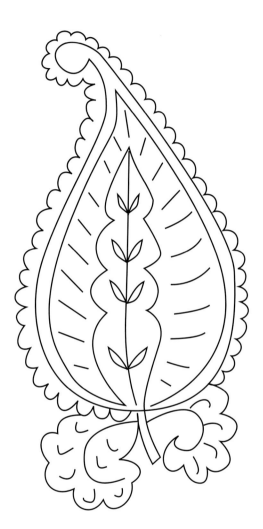

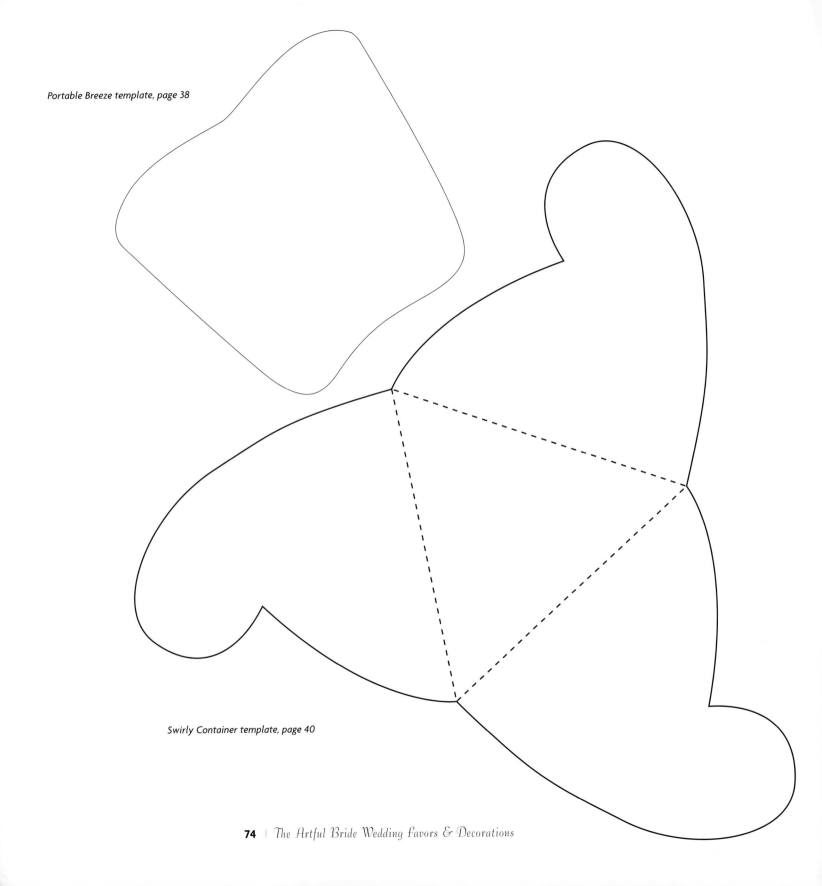

Portable Breeze template, page 38

Swirly Container template, page 40

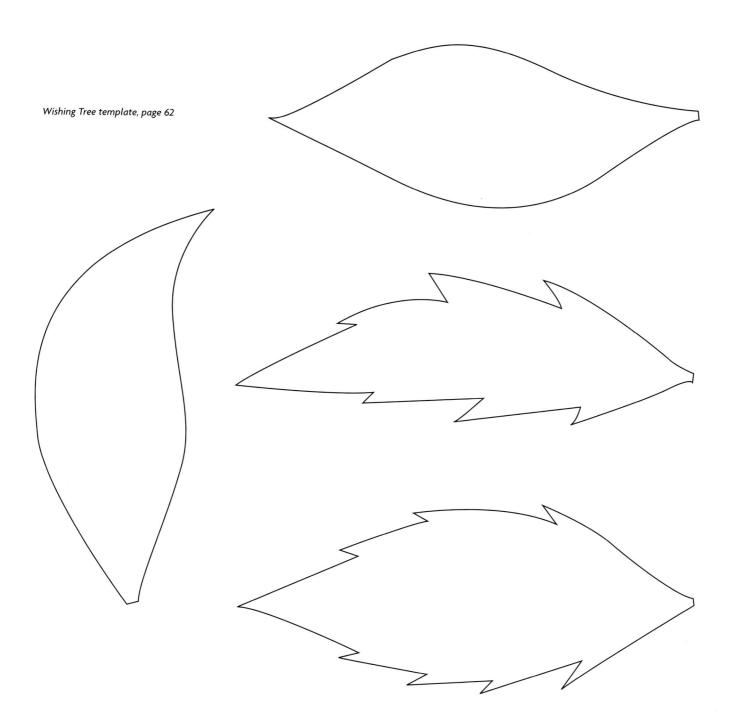

Wishing Tree template, page 62

Resources

SPECIALTY PAPERS AND SUPPLIES

Paper Source

www.paper-source.com

Locations include Chicago, Cambridge, Minneapolis, and Kansas City (check the website for other cities). Here you'll find papers of all kinds, both luxurious and simple. You'll also find adhesives, bookbinding materials, decorations, and other high-quality goods.

Kate's Paperie

561 Broadway
New York, NY 10012
www.katespaperie.com
(888) 941-9169

The landmark store is available not just to those wandering through SoHo—there are also locations in Greenwich Village, the Upper East Side, and (most importantly) online. Now you can order the exotic papers, journals, and paper accessories online or over the phone.

CRAFT SUPPLIES

Michael's

www.michaels.com

A.C. Moore

www.acmoore.com

Pearl

www.pearlpaint.com

JoAnn Fabrics

www.joann.com

BASIC BUILDING SUPPLIES

Home Depot

www.homedepot.com

Lowe's

www.lowes.com

SPECIALTY STORES AND RESOURCES

The Angelgrove Tree Seed Company

www.trees-seeds.com

Seeds to use for the Bonsai project (page 18).

Bead Works

23 Church Street

Cambridge, MA 02138

(617) 868-9777

1076 Boylston St

Boston, MA 02116

(617) 247-7227

www.beadworksboston.com

From tiny seed beads in vibrant colors to gigantic semiprecious beads, this store is likely to have it—as well as a supply of tools to finish the beading projects.

Black Ink

5 Brattle St., Harvard Square, Cambridge, MA 02139

(617) 497-1221

101 Charles Street, Boston, MA 02114

(617) 723-3883

Black Ink is a treasure trove of inspiring and useful items. From "sushi-pops" to lunch boxes and bowling ball patches, the genius behind these stores collects the best of what's out there—kitch, industrial, and elegant—for the customers who outfit their homes and projects with their goodies.

eBay

www.ebay.com

Want toys, vases, vintage Girl Scout patches, or anything else you can't seem to find in stores? Check eBay.

GetSuckered.com

www.getsuckered.com

Candy-making supplies, molds, and luster and pearl dust.

About the Authors

APRIL L. PAFFRATH is a freelance editor and writer in Cambridge, Massachusetts. In addition to book and magazine editing, she has written architecture profiles, travel pieces, cooking articles, and craft how-to's for magazines such as *Scientific American Explorations* and *Martha Stewart Living*. She is coauthor with Laura McFadden of *The Artful Bride: Simple, Handmade Wedding Projects* (Rockport, 2003).

PAULA GRASDAL is a printmaker and mixed-media artist living in Cambridge, Massachusetts. She has contributed to several Rockport publications and is coauthor, with Holly Harrison, of *Collage for the Soul: Expressing Hopes and Dreams through Art* (Rockport, 2003).

LIVIA McREE is a craft writer and designer who is always looking for new twists on beautiful crafts. She lives in Wellesley, Massachusetts, is author of four craft books, and has contributed to several others.